DUNGEONS & DRAGONS®

POCKET EXPERT

Written by Stacy King

T0190669

CONTENTS

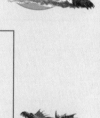

INTRODUCTION

Welcome to Faerûn, bold reader! The Forgotten Realms (as they are also called) are filled with wonder and danger. Wits and weapons will not be enough to safely travel through these lands. You'll need knowledge, too! Contained within these pages is the hard-won wisdom of monster hunters and brave explorers. Learn all about powerful magic, ferocious creatures, and dark dungeons in preparation for your own adventures.

Use the A–Z contents list above to explore topics, and check out the glossary on p.78 for any unfamiliar words.

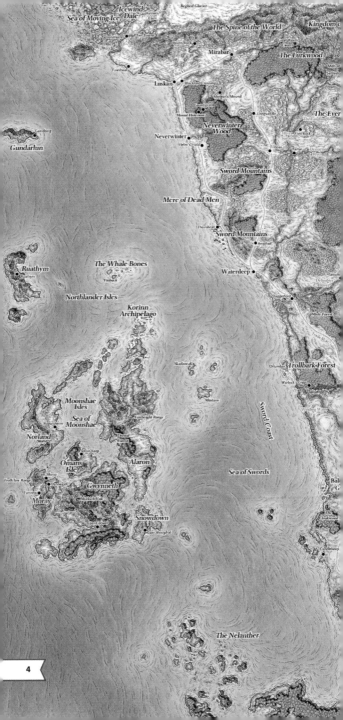

Icewind Dale
Sea of Moving Ice
Reghed Glacier
The Spine of the World
Kingdom of
Mirabar
The Lurkwood
Luskan
Mount Hotenow
Neverwinter Wood
The Ever
Neverwinter
Sword Mountains
Mere of Dead Men
Thornhold
Sword Mountains
Waterdeep
Gundarlun
Ruathym
The Whale Bones
Finback
Northlander Isles
Korinn Archipelago
Trollbark Forest
Warlock Knoll
Shalont Isle
Mintarn
Sword Coast
Moonshae Isles
Sea of Moonshae
Faelheight Range
Norland
Alaron
Sea of Swords
Omans Isle
Gwynneth
Snowdown
Moray

The Nelanther

4

WHAT IS FAERÛN?

Faerûn is a continent on the planet Toril. The continent is home to a wide variety of peoples and cultures, including humans, elves, and dwarves. The landscape includes forests, mountains, grasslands, swamps, glaciers, and ruins from long-lost kingdoms.

THE SWORD COAST

This area is dominated by city-states like Waterdeep and Baldur's Gate. The north is a range of icy mountains called the Spine of the World. Forests and hills cover the remaining land.

MOONSHAE ISLES

Located west of the Sword Coast in the Sea of Swords, each of these islands is an independent nation with a unique culture and customs.

LANDS OF INTRIGUE

These southern nations are known for their magic and mysteries. The halfling homeland of Lurien, the noble families of Amn, and the battling genies of Calimshan are found here.

5

ACERERAK

Acererak travels across dimensions, seeking souls to feed his magic. He builds dungeons full of treasure to trap adventurers. His power and cruelty make him a threat to Faerûn and beyond.

DATA FILE

PLACE OF ORIGIN Unknown

LINEAGE Half-human, half-demon

HEIGHT 6 ft (1.83 m)

CLASS Undead wizard

FAVORED ATTACK Necromantic spells

Staff of the Forgotten One

Necklace creates sphere of annihilation

Paralyzing touch

LICH

Acererak is a lich—a mortal spellcaster who used dark magic to become undead. He can reform his body if it is destroyed.

BAHAMUT

Bahamut is the god of metallic dragons and is known as the Platinum Dragon. He enjoys visiting the mortal realm in disguise. He rarely interferes in mortal affairs, except to stop his foe and sister, Tiamat.

AT A GLANCE
- ☑ Multiple attacks
- ☑ Shapechanging
- ☑ Damage immunity
- ☑ Breath weapon

DATA FILE

PLACE OF ORIGIN
Material Plane

LINEAGE Founder, metallic dragon line

FAVORED ATTACK Bite

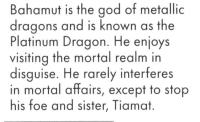

Platinum fire breath

Wingspan more than 100 ft (30 m)

Razor-sharp claws

MANY FACES

Bahamut can shape-shift. He often travels as a peasant man surrounded by seven canaries, who are gold dragons in disguise.

BALDUR'S GATE

Baldur's Gate is the largest city on the Sword Coast. Goods from all over are traded here. The Lower City is rough and dangerous. Wealthy people and noble families live in the well-guarded Upper City.

DATA FILE

REGION The Sword Coast

POPULATION 125,000 people

GOVERNMENT Council of Four Dukes

ALLIES The Lords' Alliance

Ramazith's wizard tower

Six gates give access to Upper City

Wall dividing Upper and Lower City

THE LORDS' ALLIANCE

This group of city-states located along the Sword Coast are pledged to help each other in times of danger.

BEHOLDERS

These huge floating eyeballs are hard to sneak up on. They even sleep with most of their eyes open. Proud and greedy, beholders hate most other creatures—including other beholders.

AT A GLANCE
- ☑ Magic rays
- ☑ Antimagic cone
- ☑ Alert
- ☑ Levitation

DATA FILE

TYPE Aberration

LAIR Solitary caverns

DIAMETER Approximately 10 ft (3 m)

FAVORED ATTACK Bite, magic rays

One of 10 eye stalks

Large eye blocks magic attacks

EYE RAYS

Each eye stalk shoots a different type of magic ray, including ones that can damage, frighten, or disintegrate targets.

BRUENOR BATTLEHAMMER

AT A GLANCE
- ☑ Axe wielding
- ☑ Weapons forging
- ☑ Loyalty
- ☑ Leadership

Bruenor is a valiant defender of the dwarves. He is famous for both his fighting skills and his stern temper. Beneath his gruff exterior is a courageous and caring heart.

DATA FILE

PLACE OF ORIGIN
Mithral Hall

LINEAGE Shield dwarf

HEIGHT 4 ft 6 in (1.37 m)

CLASS Fighter

FAVORED ATTACK Flaming one-handed axe

Flametongue is Bruenor's magic axe

DEFENDER OF MITHRAL HALL

Mithral Hall is an ancient dwarven stronghold. Bruenor spent years fighting the evil shadow dragon Shimmergloom to reclaim it and eventually becomes its king.

CANDLEKEEP

The massive fortress of Candlekeep contains the largest library in Faerûn. It is a center for knowledge and learning of all kinds. Magical defenses protect the books from fire and theft.

DATA FILE

REGION The Sword Coast

POPULATION 500 people

GOVERNMENT The Avowed, a religious order

ALLIES The Lords' Alliance

Great Library

Protective walls

Only one gate entrance

ENDLESS KNOWLEDGE

To gain entry, visitors must donate a book not already in the library. Recipes and diaries are shelved alongside magical tomes and historical documents.

WHO LIVES IN FAERÛN?

Faerûn is home to a wide variety of peoples and cultures. Some people travel and mingle widely, while others live in more isolated communities. Large cities tend to be the most diverse.

DRAGONBORN

Dragonborn are the proud descendants of ancient dragons. They stand almost 7 ft (2.13 m) tall and are covered in scales.

DWARVES

Dwarves are skilled fighters, miners, and crafters. They live up to 400 years and are under 5 ft (1.52 m) tall.

ELVES

Elves are graceful, magical, and long-lived. They cherish art, music, and nature, and often live in beautiful forest villages.

GNOMES

Gnomes are joyful, energetic, and inventive. Their boundless curiosity inspires them to make the most of their five centuries of life.

HALFLINGS

Halflings are cheerful, practical, and hard-working. They value the comforts of home and family, and are under 3 ft (0.91 m) tall.

HUMANS

Humans are ambitious, adaptable, and resilient. They can be found across Faerûn and represent a wide range of cultures.

TIEFLINGS

Tieflings are humans whose ancestors bargained with devils. They are clever and self-reliant, with large horns and pointed tails.

Classes are a quick way to understand a person's skills, training, and special powers. The 12 core classes include adventurers who focus on combat, spellcasting, and a mixture of both.

Barbarians
Instinctive, primal fighters

Druids
Shapechanging nature protectors

Bards
Inspiring magical performers

Fighters
Trained soldiers

Clerics
Religious healers

Monks
Disciplined martial experts

Paladins
Warriors of faith

Rangers
Hunters and trackers

Warlocks
Powered by otherworldly forces

Rogues
Spies, thieves, and assassins

Wizards
Highly educated spellcasters

Sorcerers
Intuitive magic-users

CATTI-BRIE BATTLEHAMMER

AT A GLANCE
- ☑ Archery
- ☑ Sword fighting
- ☑ Spellcasting
- ☑ Kind
- ☑ Logical

Catti-brie is a skilled archer and magic-user. She is the adopted daughter of Bruenor. She fights alongside her husband Drizzt Do'Urden using her elven bow, quiver, and the sentient sword Khazid'hea.

Quiver of Anariel

ARCANE TALENTS

Catti-brie is a powerful spellcaster. She can heal others and transform herself into different animal shapes, including eagle, owl, and wolf forms.

DATA FILE

PLACE OF ORIGIN
Icewind Dale

LINEAGE Human

HEIGHT 5 ft 5 in (1.65 m)

CLASS Fighter/wizard

FAVORED ATTACK Bow, fireball spell

Magic elven bow named Heartseeker

CULT OF THE DRAGON

This secret cult worships evil dragons and hopes to restore the Age of Dragons. They plan to free Tiamat from imprisonment using the magical powers of the five dragon masks.

Mask to hide identity

Dragon details in clothing

DATA FILE

MISSION To free the dragon Tiamat

BASE OF OPERATIONS The Well of Dragons

MEMBERS Worshipers of Tiamat

ALLIES Chromatic dragons, kobolds

Cult jewelry

DRAGON MASKS

There are five dragon masks, one for each chromatic dragon type. They can be combined into a single item.

DEMOGORGON

AT A GLANCE
- ☑ Magic resistance
- ☑ Spellcasting
- ☑ Tentacles
- ☑ Two heads
- ☑ Stunning gaze

Demogorgon is the Prince of Demons and the embodiment of chaos. His body is a meld of ape, lizard, and tentacled monstrosity. Only the bravest can resist his evil gaze.

DATA FILE

PLACE OF ORIGIN Beyond recorded history

TYPE Fiend

LAIR The Abyss

HEIGHT 18 ft (5.5 m)

FAVORED ATTACK Tentacle lash

Right head: Hathradiah

Left head: Aameul

10 ft (3 m) attack range

DOUBLE TROUBLE

Both of Demogorgon's heads can stun and confuse with their stare. They have different personalities and often disagree.

DISPLACER BEASTS

These six-legged creatures are very intelligent predators. They project a displacement illusion that hides their true location, making them hard to target. Like cats, they enjoy toying with their prey.

AT A GLANCE
- ☑ Displacement magic
- ☑ Tentacles
- ☑ Smart
- ☑ Swift

PRIZED PETS

Some people seek out displacer beast cubs, hoping to raise a loyal pet. This rarely works!

DATA FILE

PLACE OF ORIGIN The Feywild

TYPE Monstrosity

LAIR Dense forests

LENGTH 9 ft (2.7 m)

FAVORED ATTACK Ambush

Spike pads

Sleek fur

DRAGONS— CHROMATIC

There are five main types of chromatic dragon: black, blue, green, red, and white. They are selfish, evil, and greedy. Dragon lairs are well-guarded and filled with treasure.

Powerful wings

Thick protective scales

DATA FILE

TYPE Dragon

LAIR Dangerous and remote areas

LENGTH 12–30 ft+ (3.7–9 m+), depending on age

FAVORED ATTACK Magical breath weapon

DRAGON GROWTH

Dragons hatch from eggs and keep growing all their lives. Ancient dragons are thousands of years old and over 100 ft (30 m) long.

DRAGONS— METALLIC

Metallic dragons come in five types: brass, bronze, copper, gold, and silver. They are noble, curious, and protective of the innocent. They have long memories and collect treasures with personal meaning.

AT A GLANCE
- ☑ Protective scales
- ☑ Bite, claw, and tail attacks
- ☑ Intimidating
- ☑ Breath weapon
- ☑ Shapechanger

GUARDIANS

Gold dragons watch over the realms. They sometimes use their shapechanging ability to secretly investigate evil activity among mortals.

Wing attacks push away foes

DATA FILE

TYPE Dragon

LAIR Dangerous and remote areas

LENGTH 12–30 ft+ (3.7–9 m+), depending on age

FAVORED ATTACK Magical breath weapon

Sharp claws to slash enemies

WHAT POWERS DO DRAGONS HAVE?

Each type of dragon is unique, but they share some common powers. Even wyrmlings—baby dragons—can be dangerous. As dragons age, their strength and abilities also increase.

BREATH WEAPON

The most feared of a dragon's abilities is their breath weapon. This power lets them exhale a magical attack from their mouth. Chromatic dragons have one type of weapon, while metallic dragons have two.

CHROMATIC BREATH ATTACKS

Dragon Type	Weapon Type
Black	Acid
Blue	Lightning
Green	Poison
Red	Fire
White	Cold

METALLIC BREATH ATTACKS

Dragon Type	Weapon Type
Brass	Fire, Sleep
Bronze	Lightning, Repulsion
Copper	Acid, Slowing
Gold	Fire, Weakening
Silver	Cold, Paralyzing

DAMAGE IMMUNITY

A dragon cannot be hurt by any attack that matches its own breath weapon. For example, red and gold dragons are immune to fire damage.

MULTIPLE ATTACKS

In the time most creatures need for a single movement, a dragon can make three separate attacks with its bite and claws.

WING ATTACK

A dragon can beat its wings, creating a gust of wind that can damage enemies and knock them off their feet.

FRIGHTFUL PRESENCE

Dragons can deliberately try to scare nearby creatures. Frightened enemies will find it harder to move or attack.

DRIZZT DO'URDEN

AT A GLANCE
- ☑ Empathy
- ☑ Problem-solving
- ☑ Hunting and tracking
- ☑ Wilderness survival

Drizzt was raised in the Underdark by drow elves who worship the goddess Lolth. He rejected their evil and fled to the surface, where he fights injustice. His companions include Catti-brie and Bruenor Battlehammer.

Unicorn pendant

PANTHER SIDEKICK

Guenhwyvar is a loyal friend and a powerful fighter. Drizzt summons her from the Astral Plane using an onyx figurine.

DATA FILE

PLACE OF ORIGIN
Menzoberranzan

LINEAGE Drow elf

HEIGHT 5 ft 4 in (1.63 m)

CLASS Ranger

FAVORED ATTACK
Dual-wielding scimitars

Icingdeath

Twinkle

DUKE ZALTO

Duke Zalto's goal is to find and repair an ancient dragon-slaying weapon, the Vonindod. He intends to become the ruler of all giants by waging war against dragonkind.

AT A GLANCE
- ☑ Fire immunity
- ☑ Multiple attacks
- ☑ Perceptive
- ☑ Blacksmith
- ☑ Huge height

Thick plate armor

COMPANIONS

Zalto keeps two ferocious hell hounds, named Narthor and Zerebor, as pets. They hunt together and can breathe fire.

Fire-red hair

DATA FILE

PLACE OF ORIGIN
Northern Faerûn

LINEAGE Fire giant

HEIGHT 20 ft (6.1 m)

FAVORED ATTACK Giant iron maul

The Emerald Enclave fights against threats to the natural world. Their members are scattered across Faerûn, often working alone. Members are skilled in survival, fighting, and wilderness lore.

Dressed in colors of nature

Pouch equipped for survival

Repaired clothing

BALANCE

The Emerald Enclave seeks to maintain a healthy balance between civilization and the wild. Their symbol is a green stag.

FAR LANDS

LOCATION

Little is known about the most distant regions of Faerûn. Travelers tell of the sweeping desert of Zakhara, the eastern empires of Kara-Tur, and the unknown isles of the Trackless Sea.

Buildings carved into cliff face

Unique plants and creatures

MYSTERIOUS MAGIC

Even magic works differently in the far lands. The spellcasters of Zakhara draw on the magic of genies, for example.

DATA FILE

REGION East and South of Faerûn

POPULATION Unknown

GOVERNMENT Unknown

ALLIES Unknown

GAUNTLGRYM

Gauntlgrym is prized for its valuable mines and raging forge. Its ancient stones have seen empires rise and fall. Recently, Bruenor Battlehammer and his allies reclaimed the city from the drow elves of Menzoberranzan.

KEY FACTS

REGION The Crag Mountains, Northern Faerûn

POPULATION About 10,000–15,000 people

GOVERNMENT Dwarven kingdom

ALLIES Mithral Hall

Glow of heat

MAEGERA

The Great Forge burns incredibly hot because the fire elemental is trapped inside. Duke Zalto wants to steal Maegera for his own forge, Ironslag.

Wide bridges for enchanted mining carts to travel

GELATINOUS CUBES

AT A GLANCE
- ☑ See-through
- ☑ Acid attacks
- ☑ Sticky
- ☑ Sturdy

These gooey cubes may be slow, but they are deadly predators. They engulf passing creatures and dissolve them. Bones and metal are left behind, suspended in transparent ooze.

FLOATING TREASURE

A well-fed gelatinous cube can be spotted by the gems, coins, and other items suspended inside.

Last week's dinner

Gooey liquid

DATA FILE

TYPE Ooze

LAIR Dungeon hallways

SIZE 6–10 ft (1.8–3 m)

FAVORED ATTACK Engulf

29

Giants once ruled over Faerûn. Conflicts with dragons caused their empires to fall. Now they live in small clans scattered across the land.

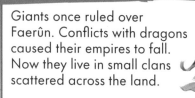

CLOUD GIANT

Affluent and clever spellcasters. They reside in airy castles on top of high mountains or magical solid clouds.

Can transform into mist

Trophies from fallen foes

FROST GIANT

Fierce warriors who relish ice and snow. They value physical strength and survive by raiding for food and treasure.

Powerful plate armor

FIRE GIANT

Master craftspeople who excel at battle. Fire giants are famed for their military tactics and mighty weapons.

DID YOU KNOW?
Giant society is organized by a system of social rank called the ordning.

Simple clothes and weapons

HILL GIANT
Simple brutes who enjoy eating and smashing. The lowest of the ordning, they get by on size and strength.

STONE GIANT
Reclusive artists and dreamers. These giants dwell in quiet caves where they can focus on their stone carving.

Heavy club

Giant-sized greatsword

Can breathe water and air

STORM GIANT
Solitary thinkers who live isolated lives. They are wise and peaceful, but also dangerous when angered.

GOBLINS

AT A GLANCE
- ☑ Nimble
- ☑ Pack hunters
- ☑ Ambushers
- ☑ Trap-makers

Goblins are small, mean creatures who rely on pack tactics and overwhelming numbers to win battles. Their lairs are filled with narrow tunnels and traps to keep out larger foes.

WORG RIDERS

Some goblins ride wolves or their larger cousins, worgs, when hunting. These dangerous creatures will turn on their riders if mistreated.

Sees through darkness

DATA FILE

TYPE Goblinoid

LAIR Caves and tunnels

HEIGHT 3 ft 5 in (1 m)

FAVORED ATTACK Scimitar, shortbow

Rusted gear

A party is a group of adventurers who have joined forces—either for a single mission or as a lifelong alliance. Most parties include people from several different classes.

QUESTS

A party's specific goals—such as rescuing a kidnapped person or fighting a monster—are known as quests.

RANGE OF SKILLS

A party must be ready for all kinds of dangers. Their combined abilities should include healing, fighting, wilderness survival, magic, and investigation.

TRUSTED ALLIES

Party members are often friends—but even enemies can work together against a common foe. Trust is essential for a party's success!

WHY DO PEOPLE BECOME ADVENTURERS?

Adventurers come from a wide array of backgrounds—with different upbringings, education, and interests. There are many reasons for taking this dangerous yet exciting path. But the one thing adventurers have in common is the courage to act when needed!

BORN FOR IT

A few people are born with a prophecy, a curse, or some other factor that cannot be resisted. Such people become adventurers whether they want to or not.

EARLY TRAINING

Some adventurers are educated in their skills from a young age. Fighters, monks, and wizards can spend years studying their craft before joining a party.

ACT OF FAITH

Religious duty is a common inspiration for clerics and paladins, but they are not the only ones. Belief in a higher purpose can help when facing tough challenges.

FAME AND GLORY

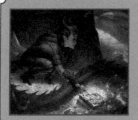

Treasure, respect, or a statue of themselves in the city center—an adventuring life offers many rewards for those who survive the dangers.

NECESSITY

Some people who never dreamed of adventuring find themselves with no choice when their home and family are threatened.

Most people in Faerûn work as farmers, hunters, craftspeople, or merchants. Their attitudes toward adventurers can range from admiration to distrust.

HALASTER BLACKCLOAK

AT A GLANCE
- ☑ Spellcasting
- ☑ Teleportation
- ☑ Shapechanger
- ☑ Regeneration

Halaster Blackcloak is a master of magic gates. He frequently moves the monsters and traps in his dungeon, Undermountain. He prefers to remain unseen, using spells to observe adventurers.

DATA FILE

PLACE OF ORIGIN
Waterdeep

LINEAGE Human

CLASS Wizard

FAVORED ATTACK
Lightning bolt

Blast scepter

Robe of eyes

MAGICAL ITEMS

Halaster wears a robe of eyes that lets him see in all directions. His staff is a blast scepter that pushes away foes.

HARPERS

Harpers are secret agents who rely on knowledge and investigation to fight injustice. They are trained to act alone and use force only as a last resort.

Watchful gaze

MUSICAL SECRETS

Harpers use music to communicate secretly with one another. Their emblem is a harp within a crescent moon.

Hidden emblem inside cloak

DATA FILE

MISSION To protect the common folk

BASE OF OPERATIONS The Sword Coast

MEMBERS Bards, rogues, spies

ALLIES Emerald Enclave

ICEWIND DALE

Icewind Dale is the northernmost region of the Sword Coast. Ten small towns exist amid the ice and snow. The wilderness contains barbarian tribes, dwarven miners, and cold-loving monsters.

FROZEN WILDS

Icewind Dale's rocky mountains have plenty of space for large creatures like frost giants, mammoths, and white dragons.

Snowstorms can hide dangers

DATA FILE

REGION Northern Sword Coast

POPULATION 4,200 people

GOVERNMENT Local councils

ALLIES Luskan, Zhentarim

Torches provide light and heat

Warm clothes required!

ILLITHIDS

AT A GLANCE
- ☑ Magic resistance
- ☑ Tentacles
- ☑ Mind blast
- ☑ Telepathy

Also called mind flayers, these alien creatures can communicate telepathically and control other creatures with their powers. Their hive mind lets them organize evil plots across great distances.

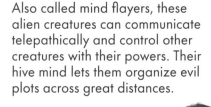

DATA FILE

TYPE Aberration
LAIR Underdark, Astral Planes
HEIGHT 6–7 ft (1.8–2.1 m)
FAVORED ATTACK Psychic

Long tentacles

DID YOU KNOW?

Mind flayer colonies are controlled by an elder brain.

INTELLECT DEVOURER

Illithids create these walking brains as servants and guards. They can sense when intelligent creatures are nearby.

Ironslag is an ancient fire giant forge able to shape magical metals. Ogres, goblins, and fire giants protect the forge's treasure—parts of the lost Vonindod mechanical device, ready for reassembly.

DATA FILE

REGION Far North

SIZE Unknown

GOVERNMENT Ruled by Duke Zalto

ALLIES Underdark drow (House Xorlarrin)

GETTING INSIDE

The doors of Ironslag are 50 ft (15 m) tall and sealed with magic. The other option is climbing up a 500 ft (152 m) cliff.

Duke Zalto towers above

Pet hell hound

Fighter in front protects the party

Spellcaster attacks from a distance

KOBOLDS

Kobolds hatch from eggs and have rust-colored scales. Individual kobolds are not physically strong, but they can overwhelm larger foes by working together.

AT A GLANCE
- ☑ Collaboration
- ☑ Pack tactics
- ☑ Trap-making
- ☑ Tunnel building
- ☑ Hiding

DATA FILE

TYPE Humanoid
LAIR Caves, dungeons
HEIGHT 2 ft 6 in (76 cm)
FAVORED ATTACK Ambushes

Sensitive to sunlight

Protective scales

Simple weapon

MIGHTY ANCESTORS

Kobolds are proud of their dragon heritage. They view evil dragons as demigods and jump at any chance to serve one.

41

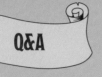
WHAT ARE THE DIFFERENT TYPES OF MAGIC?

Magic is woven through the fabric of Faerûn. There are several ways to access this power, depending on a person's training, abilities, and background.

DIVINE POWER

Clerics and paladins channel the will of the gods when performing magic. This divine gift fuels their healing spells, repels the undead, and punishes the wicked.

PACT MAGIC

A warlock's spells are powered by their patron. This otherworldly being might be a fey, demon, or other ancient entity.

KI

Through extensive training, monks can tap into ki—a mystical force that flows through living bodies. The ki lets them perform physical feats at supernatural levels.

NATURE

Druids and rangers see their magic as coming from nature. Druids draw on this wild power to speak with animals, change into beast shapes, and entangle enemies in vines.

MUSIC

Bards view words as both music and magic. Through their songs and speech, they can channel unseen vibrations to inspire and heal their allies.

DID YOU KNOW?

Magical items, potions, and spell scrolls can be used by anyone, regardless of their magical ability.

THE WEAVE

Wizards see all magic as the Weave—an unseen thread running through everything. They study extensively to learn how to access this power. Sorcerers tap into the Weave instinctually.

LUSKAN

Luskan is a bustling port town of sailors, pirates, and merchants. Its nickname is the City of Sails. Five pirate gangs, called Ships, control the city: Kurth, Baram, Suljack, Taerl, and Rethnor.

ARCANE BROTHERHOOD

This wizard group is headquartered in Hosstower, just outside Luskan. Their magical experiments are a source of worry for Luskan residents.

DATA FILE

REGION Northern Sword Coast

POPULATION About 5,000 people

GOVERNMENT High Captains of the Five Ships

ALLIES Icewind Dale, The Lords' Alliance

Hosstower

Fog and salty air are constant

MENZOBERRANZAN

Capital of the drow empire, this underground city is built into a vast cavern. The buildings are carved from stalactites and stalagmites, connected with bridges of hardened spiderweb.

DATA FILE

REGION Underdark
POPULATION 20,000+ people
GOVERNMENT Matriarchy
ALLIES Giant spiders
NICKNAME City of Shadows

Magical lights

Narbondellyn, the nobles' district

Merchants trade in the Bazaar

SPIDER CULT

Menzoberranzan is ruled by worshipers of Lolth, the goddess of spiders and lies. Those who resist her evil teachings are exiled ... or worse!

45

MIMICS

AT A GLANCE
- ☑ Shapechanger
- ☑ Sticky body
- ☑ Patient
- ☑ Cunning

Mimics can alter their form to look like almost anything. They patiently wait until their prey gets close, then they attack with their sharp teeth and huge tongue.

DATA FILE

TYPE Monstrosity
LAIR Anywhere
SIZE Variable
FAVORED ATTACK Sneak

CUNNING DISGUISE

Mimics prefer shapes that invite curiosity, like doors, bags, or treasure chests. Some mimics join together in colonies that can imitate whole villages!

Gaping jaws

Tongue grabs prey

Sticky surface traps targets

MINSC & BOO

AT A GLANCE
- ☑ Courageous
- ☑ Optimistic
- ☑ Loyal ally
- ☑ Sword fighting (just Minsc!)

Minsc is a strong, kindhearted warrior who is unrelenting in his battle against evil. He is easily confused and often takes advice from his fuzzy companion, Boo.

Two-handed sword

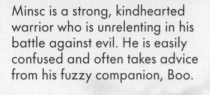

DATA FILE

PLACE OF ORIGIN
Rashemaar/Unknown

LINEAGE Human/
Unknown

HEIGHT 6 ft 3 in (1.91 m)/
3 ft (91 cm)

CLASS Ranger/Hamster

FAVORED ATTACK
Longsword/Leap

Small size perfect for spying

MAGICALLY SHRUNK?

Minsc claims Boo is a miniature giant space hamster who was shrunk by a wizard. This has never been proven.

MITHRAL HALL

Mithral Hall is a vast underground city of tunnels and carved halls. The original dwarf residents were driven out by a dragon. Bruenor Battlehammer won it back with the help of his friends.

SHIMMERGLOOM THE DRAGON

The shadow dragon Shimmergloom was set free when the dwarves dug too deep. Only 300 dwarves escaped from his attack.

Elaborate stonework

DATA FILE

REGION The Frost Hills, Northern Faerûn

POPULATION 5,000 people

GOVERNMENT Dwarven kingdom

ALLIES The Lords' Alliance

Dwarven engineering

Built to last

MORDENKAINEN

This powerful wizard is renowned across many worlds. Mordenkainen is a stern man with a piercing gaze. He constantly explores and experiments to discover new magic.

AT A GLANCE
- ☑ Spellcasting
- ☑ Intelligent
- ☑ Arcane knowledge
- ☑ Confident

Great magical understanding

DATA FILE

PLACE OF ORIGIN The planet Oerth

LINEAGE Human

HEIGHT 5 ft 11 in (1.8 m)

CLASS Wizard

FAVORED ATTACK Mordenkainen's Sword

Bracers of Defense

SPELLMAKER

Mordenkainen has invented many useful spells, most of which are named after him. Mordenkainen's Sword creates a blade of magical energy, for example.

49

Neverwinter is a bustling coastal city of talented craftspeople and skilled gardeners. It was badly damaged 50 years ago when Mount Hotenow erupted. Those who survived now work to restore the city's glory.

Castle Never

DATA FILE

REGION The Sword Coast

POPULATION 23,000 people

GOVERNMENT Regency

ALLIES The Lords' Alliance

NICKNAME The Jewel of the North

Still rebuilding damaged areas

MOUNT HOTENOW

This volcano's blazing interior makes it an ideal home for fire elementals, giants, and a red dragon named Karrundax.

OGRES

AT A GLANCE
- ☑ Huge size
- ☑ Omnivorous
- ☑ Strong
- ☑ Scary

Ogres are known for three things: size, strength, and ferocious rage. They anger quickly and often break things they don't understand. Eating and smashing stuff are their main interests.

DATA FILE

TYPE Giant

LAIR Caves, farmhouses

HEIGHT 9–10 ft (2.7–3 m)

FAVORED ATTACK Greatclub

Handmade jewelry from random junk

FASHION

Ogres can eat almost anything—moldy cheese, sheep, and even people. They are fond of making trinkets from whatever they don't consume.

Primitive handmade weapons

WHAT IS FAERÛN'S PAST?

The known history of Faerûn spans thousands of years. Its human empires are relatively new. The ruins of other, older kingdoms can be found across the land.

DAYS OF THUNDER

The first inhabitants were species with reptile, frog, and bird features. Their mighty empires ended 30,000 years ago.

DAWN AGE

In this era, powerful giants and dragons ruled the land. Over thousands of years, their constant warfare nearly led to their extinction.

THE FIRST FLOWERING

Elves and dwarves rose in power as the dragons lessened. They built strong nations across the Sword Coast.

THE CROWN WARS

A conflict of 3,000 years between the elven kingdoms led to great destruction of both land and cities. At its end, the drow elves were banished to the Underdark.

THE RISE AND FALL OF NETHERIL

The first powerful human empire, Netheril, was a place of magic and wonder. Its floating cities fell when the mage Karsus tried to overthrow Mystra, the goddess of magic.

THE GREAT CITIES

In the last 1,500 years, human cities have flourished across Faerûn. Humans and elves made alliances to ensure peace.

THE SPELLPLAGUE

The gods Cyric and Shar killed Mystra. This shattered the magical force known as the Weave, killing many people and remaking the continent. The chaos of Mystra's death and rebirth still lingers.

OWLBEARS

AT A GLANCE
- ☑ Ferocious
- ☑ Strong
- ☑ Keen senses
- ☑ Multiple attacks

These large predators have sharp beaks and equally sharp claws. Their shaggy fur is covered by feathers. Owlbears are known to be aggressive, ill-tempered, and afraid of nothing.

DATA FILE

TYPE Monstrosity

LAIR Caves, old ruins

HEIGHT 12 ft (3.7 m) or 20 ft (6.1 m) on hind legs

FAVORED ATTACK Claws and beak

Darkvision for night hunting

Thick feathers provide protection and warmth

DARK DENS

Owlbears live in caves or ruins where their eggs will be safe during their nightly hunts. The entrance is usually full of bones and bad smells!

PHANDALIN

Phandalin is a quiet town in northern Faerûn. Bandits and monsters endanger the peaceful villagers. A terrible threat is growing in the abandoned mines beneath the town.

LOST MAGIC

Phandalin was built on the ruins of an older town. Forgotten relics of dangerous power lie buried beneath.

DATA FILE

REGION Sword Mountains
POPULATION 500 people
GOVERNMENT Town council
ALLIES Neverwinter

Damaged remains of Cragmaw Castle

Houses have few defenses

RED WIZARDS OF THAY

Red wizards use undead armies to rule the land of Thay. They seek to control all of Faerûn. Magic, bribes, and blackmail are their favorite tools to corrupt local leadership.

DID YOU KNOW?

Red wizards are widely distrusted. They often disguise themselves with illusion magic when outside Thay.

DATA FILE

MISSION To spread their undead empire across Faerûn

BASE OF OPERATIONS Thay

MEMBERS Spellcasters, undead minions

ALLIES Bribed or corrupted locals

Magical staff channels powers

Enchanted armor

TATTOOS

Red wizards adorn their shaved heads with complex tattoos. The designs reflect their area of magical expertise.

RUST MONSTERS

AT A GLANCE
- ☑ Destroys metal
- ☑ Strong bite
- ☑ Sees in dark
- ☑ Tough

Rust monsters can quickly destroy an adventurer's weapons and armor. Any metal that touches them will begin to rust. The monsters then eat the remains.

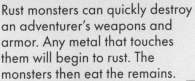

DATA FILE

TYPE Monstrosity

LAIR Underground tunnels

LENGTH 5–8 ft (1.5–2.4 m)

FAVORED ATTACK Rust metal

DROP THE SWORDS

Simple weapons like clubs, staffs, and rocks work well against rust monsters. Wood and stone can't be damaged by their corrosive skin.

Thick scales

Antenna can grab items

Can smell metal within 30 ft (9 m)

SILVER MARCHES

Dense forests and deep mines once made this region a thriving home for dwarves, elves, and humans. But recent warfare has scarred the land and shattered cities, causing many to flee.

DATA FILE

REGION Northern Faerûn

POPULATION Unknown

GOVERNMENT
Independent city-states

ALLIES None

NICKNAME Luruar

DANGEROUS ALLIES

Orc tribes often raid in this region. They allied with white dragons and frost giants in the War of the Silver Marches.

Fortress smashed by giants

Travel remains risky

Weapons of fallen armies

The Sword Coast is a large territory that includes human cities, dwarven kingdoms, and independent nations. Roads and ships allow people to trade and share information.

RISKY WATERS

Travel by sea has many dangers, including pirates, storms, and dragon turtle attacks. Rocky shorelines with high cliffs add to the peril.

Sailing ship

Coastal port

DID YOU KNOW?

Many adventurers earn coins by protecting trade goods or travelers on the Sword Coast's dangerous roads.

WHO ARE THE GODS OF FAERÛN?

Religion is part of everyday life in Faerûn. Each god and goddess has their own area of influence. Most people worship only a few gods but respect (or fear) the others. Here are some of the best known, although there are many others.

SHAR

Shar is the goddess of darkness. She is Selûne's twin sister. Like light and shadows, they are in constant conflict.

SELÛNE

Selûne is the moon goddess. One of the oldest deities, she oversees the stars, navigation, and motherhood.

DID YOU KNOW?

All of existence, including the gods, was created by Ao. As Overgod, Ao is distant from mortal affairs and rarely worshiped.

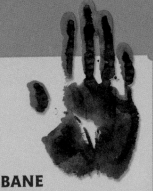

DID YOU KNOW?

In Faerûn, gods are expected to answer requests from their faithful. An unresponsive deity will lose both worshipers and power.

BANE

Bane is the god of tyranny. He represents ambition, control, and the rule of the strong.

LATHANDER

Lathander is the god of the dawn. He represents spring, rebirth, and renewal. His colors are red and gold.

TYR

Tyr is the god of justice. His followers are sworn to uphold honesty, truth, and the punishment of wrongdoers.

MYSTRA

Mystra is the goddess of magic. She controls the Weave, which allows mortal spellcasters to use magic safely.

SZASS TAM

AT A GLANCE
- ☑ Necromancy
- ☑ Rejuvenation
- ☑ Knowledgeable
- ☑ Army of loyal undead

Szass Tam is a powerful lich and the Regent of Thay. He despises all living creatures. His goal is to make everyone in Faerûn into his undead servants.

Necromancy symbol

DATA FILE

PLACE OF ORIGIN Thay

LINEAGE Human

HEIGHT 6 ft (1.83 m)

CLASS Undead wizard

FAVORED ATTACK Undead army

Magical Red Wizard robes

BECKONING DEATH

Szass Tam uses this spell to transform many residents of Thay into undead zombies who must obey his commands.

TARRASQUE

Perhaps the most feared monster in Faerûn, a tarrasque can swallow creatures whole and crush buildings underfoot. Its scaly hide resists both magic and nonmagical attacks.

AT A GLANCE
- ☑ Huge size
- ☑ Reflective scales
- ☑ Frightful presence
- ☑ Multiple attacks

Frightens enemies

Does extra damage to buildings

DATA FILE

TYPE Monstrosity

LAIR Unknown

SIZE Gargantuan! 50 ft (15.2 m) tall and 70 ft (21.3 m) long

FAVORED ATTACK Claws, fangs, and tail

SUMMONING SCROLL

A tarrasque can be called using magic scrolls. However, it will attack everything—including the summoner!

TASHA

AT A GLANCE
- ☑ Magic resistance
- ☑ Spellcasting
- ☑ Fey magic
- ☑ Immortal

Tasha was raised by Baba Yaga, the mother of all witches. Tasha is a powerful magician who has lived in many dimensions, including the Feywild. She and Mordenkainen are friendly rivals.

Tasha's Feywild home, the Palace of Heart's Desire

DATA FILE

PLACE OF ORIGIN
The planet Oerth

LINEAGE Human

HEIGHT 5 ft 6 in (1.68 m)

CLASS Wizard and archfey

FAVORED ATTACK
Tasha's Hideous Laughter

DID YOU KNOW?
Tasha goes by many names, including Iggwilv the Witch Queen and Zybilna the Archfey.

Enchanted throne shouts if anyone else sits on it

LAUGHING SPELL

Tasha's signature spell causes a person to be overcome by laughter, and so unable to attack or defend themselves.

TEMPLE OF ELEMENTAL EVIL

Four cults operate in the Sumber Hills, and each controls a different abandoned castle. Beneath the hills is the Temple of Elemental Evil. If unleashed, the temple's ancient magic could devastate Faerûn.

DATA FILE

REGION Northern Faerûn

SIZE Unknown

CREATED BY The Elder Elemental Eye

INHABITANTS Cultists, elemental creatures

HIDDEN CULTS

Each of the four cults worships a different elemental power: air, earth, fire, and water. Their magic is based on their element.

Magical trident

Shield blocks bite attack

Giant crocodile

Green energy of necromantic spell

TIAMAT

Ancient and powerful, Tiamat is the mother of chromatic dragons and first of their kind. Her brother Bahamut is her rival. Each of her five heads has a unique personality, but all are greedy, cruel, and unforgiving.

DATA FILE

PLACE OF ORIGIN
Material Plane

LINEAGE
Founder, chromatic dragon line

HEIGHT Variable

CLASS
Dragon queen

FAVORED ATTACK
Five different breath weapons

Bite can frighten opponents

Heads act independently

IMPRISONED

Tiamat has been imprisoned in Avernus, a hell dimension. She can only leave when summoned by a complex ritual.

TOMB OF ANNIHILATION

This dungeon is hidden on a jungle island. Acererak built it to trap the souls of fallen adventurers. Its many traps and secret doors are maintained by undead guardians.

FABLED TREASURES

Acererak filled the tomb with riches to tempt explorers. So far, no one has survived to claim these rewards.

Filled with complex riddles and traps

Hidden doors and fake entrances to confuse adventurers

DATA FILE

REGION
The Sea of Swords

SIZE Unknown

CREATED BY Acererak

INHABITANTS Undead dwarves, skeletons, a beholder

NICKNAME
Tomb of Horrors

WHAT SHOULD YOU BRING TO A DUNGEON?

Preparation is an important part of a successful adventure. There are no convenience stores in dungeons, so a party needs to bring along everything they will need to survive.

Mace of smiting

Dwarven warhammer

MELEE WEAPONS

These weapons are used for up-close fighting. There are many options, including daggers, swords, axes, maces, and warhammers.

RANGED WEAPONS

When fighting enemies at a distance, ranged weapons are key—from simple spears and slingshots to elegant bows and finely balanced javelins.

PROTECTIVE GEAR

Armor, shields, helmets, and boots help protect from enemy attacks and other dangers, like falling rocks and stormy weather.

MAGICAL SUPPLIES

Many spells require physical components, like flower petals or small gems, which are used up when the spell is cast.

FOOD

It isn't easy to find a good meal in a dungeon. Packing trail rations like dried meat, nuts, fruit, and water is vital.

Navigation tool

DUNGEONEER TOOLS

A compass, rope, torches, lockpicking kits, and iron spikes for climbing walls are helpful for overcoming dungeon obstacles.

BACKPACK AND BEDROLL

Sleeping on stone floors is easier with a bedroll or other soft surface. A sturdy backpack will carry everything, including treasure, on the way out.

UNDERDARK

This massive network of caves, caverns, and underground waterways lies miles below the surface of Faerûn. It is home to many strange creatures and societies, including drow elves, deep gnomes, and duergar dwarves.

DID YOU KNOW?

There are many different passages between the Underdark and the surface lands.

Vast caverns

DATE FILE

REGION Underground
SIZE Unknown
KEY CITIES Menzoberranzan, Gracklstugh
NICKNAME The Realms Below

Light travels

Glowing mushrooms

MYCONID

These intelligent fungi look like colorful walking mushrooms. They live in colonies and communicate using telepathic spores.

UNDERMOUNTAIN

Undermountain is the largest, deepest dungeon in Faerûn. It contains more than 20 interconnected levels. Different kinds of monsters, traps, and treasure can be found on each level.

DATE FILE

REGION Inside Mount Waterdeep

SIZE 20+ levels

CREATED BY Halaster Blackcloak

ALLIES None

INHABITANTS Giant animals, serpent people, evil mages

Magic keeps pillars and ceilings from collapsing

Patrolling monsters

Teamwork needed for survival

THE YAWNING PORTAL

A retired adventurer named Durnan built an inn over the dungeon's entrance. He will offer advice to explorers—for a price!

VECNA

Vecna was once a mortal spellcaster. He used dark magic to transform himself into an archlich—a powerful undead wizard. If his body is destroyed, he can create a new one.

DATA FILE

PLACE OF ORIGIN The planet Oerth

LINEAGE Human

HEIGHT 6 ft 3 in (1.91 m)

CLASS Undead wizard

FAVORED ATTACK Life drain, zombies

Undead body

Spellbook

BOOK OF VILE DARKNESS

This spellbook records Vecna's dark magic and vile knowledge. Other artifacts include his eye and hand, which provide power but corrupt all who use them.

WATERDEEP

The largest city on the Sword Coast, Waterdeep is a peaceful yet bustling city. The City Watch keeps the streets safe, while the Griffon Cavalry patrols above on their winged mounts.

Griffon Cavalry

DATA FILE

REGION The Sword Coast
POPULATION 2,000,000+
GOVERNMENT Council of Lords
ALLIES The Lords' Alliance
NICKNAME City of Splendors

Palace of Waterdeep

MYSTICAL LEADERSHIP

Laeral Silverhand is the current Lord of Waterdeep. She is one of seven daughters of Mystra, the goddess of magic.

WELL OF DRAGONS

Dragons have been coming to the top of this extinct volcano to die for thousands of years. The Cult of the Dragon plans to raise Tiamat's Temple within this dragon graveyard.

DATA FILE

REGION Central Faerûn

SIZE Unknown

CREATED BY Dragons

INHABITANTS Cultists, giants, chromatic dragons

NICKNAME The Graveyard of Dragons

DRAAKHORN

Tiamat made this horn to warn dragons of danger. It can be heard by those up to 2,000 miles (3,218 km) away. The cult hopes it will summon her supporters to the well.

Territorial dragons attack intruders

Resting place of ancient dragons

Temple of Tiamat

WITCHLIGHT CARNIVAL

The Witchlight Carnival is an interdimensional circus that visits Faerûn every eight years. Visitors can enjoy magical games, rides, and performances. Careless visitors may find themselves unable to ever leave.

DATA FILE

REGION Outside cities around Faerûn

SIZE Unknown

CREATED BY Mister Witch and Mister Light

STAFF Fairies, elves, giant snails

Performances mix illusion magic and real danger

Striped tent

Colorful fire-breather costume

FAIRY TRICKS

Many of the circus staff are fairy creatures. A one-way portal to the Feywild, the fairy realm, lies hidden among the tents.

75

XANATHAR

AT A GLANCE
- ☑ Perceptive
- ☑ Paranoid
- ☑ Minions
- ☑ Vast wealth

Xanathar is a crime lord who lives in Skullport, a hidden cavern beneath Waterdeep. Like all beholders, he is very greedy. He only cares for gold and his pet fish, Sylgar.

DATA FILE

PLACE OF ORIGIN
Astral Plane

LINEAGE Beholder

DIAMETER 15 ft (4.6 m)

FAVORED ATTACK
Petrification ray

SOMETHING'S FISHY

Beholders have long lives. Goldfish do not. Luckily for his staff, Xanathar can't tell one fish from another.

Watches for spies and traitors

Constantly reads to gain new information

ZHENTARIM

In public, the Zhentarim are respectable mercenaries for hire. Behind the scenes, they are a shadowy criminal organization—determined to build influence and power at any cost.

AT A GLANCE
- ✓ Vast network
- ✓ Secretive
- ✓ Tight-knit
- ✓ Capable fighters

One-sided cape

BADGE OF LOYALTY

The symbol of the Zhentarim is a winged serpent. This design appears on their weapon hilts and jewelry.

DATA FILE

MISSION To gather power

BASE OF OPERATIONS The Sword Coast

MEMBERS Fighters, thieves, corrupt bankers, officials

ALLIES Anyone they can pay off

Concealed weapons

GLOSSARY

ABERRATION
An alien monster that often has magical abilities.

ARCANE
Secret and mysterious; often used to describe magic.

ARCHFEY
An exceptionally powerful fey.

ARCHLICH
An exceptionally powerful lich.

CITY-STATE
A city with its own government that is not part of a larger nation.

CORROSIVE
Able to gradually weaken or destroy.

CULTIST
A member of a small religious group that is sometimes considered strange or dangerous.

DARKVISION
The ability to see shades of gray in complete darkness.

DEITIES
Gods and goddesses, beings with divine or supernatural powers.

DISPLACEMENT
When something is moved out of its proper or usual place.

ELEMENTAL
A magical creature made from a specific element, like fire, water, air, or earth.

ENGULF
To flow over and around something, and so completely cover it.

FEY
A magical fairy creature with close ties to nature.

FEYWILD
A realm where the fey live.

FIEND
A devil or demon.

FORGE
A place used by blacksmiths to heat metal into different shapes.

GREATSWORD
A long, heavy sword that must be held in both hands when used.

HIVE MIND
A group of individuals who are controlled by a single mind or awareness.

HUMANOID
A class of creatures with a humanlike body shape.

ILLUSION
Magic that tricks the senses into seeing things that aren't really there.

IMMUNITY
Protection from negative effects.

INTUITIVE
Able to quickly understand something without relying on careful thought.

LICH
An undead wizard.

LORE
Knowledge, often gained through study or experience.

MAGE
A magic-user.

MATRIARCHY
A society ruled by women.

MERCENARIES
Fighters who provide their services in exchange for money.

MONSTROSITY
An unnatural creature, often weird and dangerous.

NECROMANCY
Using dark magic to contact, control, or raise the dead.

OMNIVOROUS
Able to eat anything, including meat and plants.

ONYX
A gemstone with a bright sheen. Often connected to sadness or bad luck.

PERCEPTIVE
Observant and wise; able to notice important and often small details.

PREDATORS
Creatures who survive by hunting and eating others.

RECLUSIVE
Withdrawn or detached from society.

REJUVENATION
A magical effect that creates a new body to replace one that has been destroyed.

REPULSION
A magical effect that pushes away the targeted person or creature.

SCIMITARS
Relatively light swords with a curved blade.

SENTIENT
Able to sense and feel.

SPELLCASTING
Using magic to create a single, specific effect, such as throwing a ball of fire or turning invisible.

STRONGHOLD
A structure that is built with protective features to keep out intruders.

TELEPORTATION
Moving a person, creature, or object from one location to another instantly.

TOMES
Books, often large and covering serious topics.

UNDEAD
Creatures who have died and been revived using dark magic.

DK | Penguin Random House

Senior Editor Ruth Amos
Project Art Editor Stefan Georgiou
Production Editor Siu Yin Chan
Senior Production Controller Laura Andrews
Managing Editor Rachel Lawrence
Managing Art Editor Vicky Short
Managing Director Mark Searle

Designed for DK by Ala Uddin
US Proofreader Kayla Dugger

First American Edition, 2024
Published in the United States by DK Publishing,
a division of Penguin Random House LLC
1745 Broadway, 20th Floor, New York, NY 10019

Page design copyright © 2024 Dorling Kindersley Limited
24 25 26 27 28 10 9 8 7 6 5 4 3 2 1
001–340900–Oct/2024

A catalog record for this book
is available from the Library of Congress.
ISBN 978-0-7440-9904-1

DK books are available at special discounts when purchased
in bulk for sales promotions, premiums, fund-raising, or educational use.
For details, contact: DK Publishing Special Markets,
1745 Broadway, 20th Floor, New York, NY 10019
SpecialSales@dk.com

Printed and bound in China

www.dk.com
dnd.wizards.com

MIX
Paper | Supporting
responsible forestry
FSC™ C018179

This book was made with Forest
Stewardship Council™ certified
paper—one small step in DK's
commitment to a sustainable future.
Learn more at **www.dk.com/uk/
information/sustainability**